Wild, Wild Weather

Written by Hannah Reed
Series Consultant: Linda Hoyt

T0359742

WorldWise™
Content-based Learning

Contents

Chapter 1

Way-out weather

Weather helps keep all living things on Earth alive. It brings wind and rain, warmth and coolness. But weather changes all the time, and when it is extreme, it can kill.

Wind can form raging hurricanes that rip up trees, blow away cars and demolish houses. It can twist into tornadoes that suck up everything in their path. The wind can also whip up sandstorms and dust storms. These storms make breathing nearly impossible and bury cars and buildings.

During thunderstorms, lightning can start **bushfires** and strike buildings and people, and pelting rain can wash away houses and start mudslides.

Extreme temperatures can kill. Living things have a difficult time surviving intense heat or cold. People die in heat waves every summer. In winter, snow and ice storms bring freezing temperatures and can cause trees and electrical wires to collapse.

Storms at sea can sink ships and send huge waves crashing onto the shore, flooding the land with salty water.

Some of the worst disasters people have lived through have been caused by wild, wild weather.

Find out more

The Lut Desert in Iran holds the record for the hottest place on Earth. In 2005, the temperature reached 70 degrees Celsius. The coldest temperature ever recorded was in Antarctica in 1983: –89 degrees Celsius.

The wettest place on Earth is Mawsynram in India, which has an average annual rainfall of more than 1,187 centimetres. Nearby, the town of Cherrapunji holds the record for the most rainfall in one year: over 2,540 centimetres. Find out about weather records where you live, e.g. the hottest day, the coldest day.

5

Meteorologist and storm chaser

My name is Stan, and I am a **meteorologist**. My interest in meteorology began when I was nearly struck by lightning on the way home from school. I was only ten years old. The lightning hit the ground so close to me that my hair stood on end and I heard loud clicking noises. The next thing I knew, I was lying on the ground.

As you can imagine, this incident gave me a big scare. But what had happened was also fascinating to me. Where did the storm come from? How did the lightning work? It was the beginning of my interest in weather, particularly wild weather and storms. Today, I'm a meteorologist who specialises in understanding storms.

In my work, I follow storms on a computer and look at the data gathered from weather stations all over the country. I use the data to analyse what a storm is doing, how big it is, and where it is likely to travel, and then to make predictions about how it will develop. The information I provide helps others at my work to give warnings to the public and to ensure that people take action to be safe during storms.

I enjoy my job, but occasionally I miss the excitement of the work I used to do when I first started as a meteorologist. I used to be a storm chaser. Back then, the only way to really know what was happening in a hurricane was to fly into the middle of the storm as it gathered over the sea and collect information.

Flying into a hurricane was very noisy and bumpy, until we reached the centre, a place called the eye, where suddenly everything was very quiet and still.

The plane carried instruments to measure a hurricane's wind speed and **air pressure**. We might have to fly through the hurricane six or seven times before we had collected all of the data that we needed.

The view from the cockpit, flying into the eye of a hurricane.

At the time, people thought I was foolish to get into an aeroplane that flew straight into a storm. But they didn't understand that we were extremely careful to be as safe as possible. The pilot was trained to fly in extreme weather conditions, and the plane had been specially built to withstand hailstones and lightning strikes.

The work we did in storm chasing saved lives because we were able to give accurate warnings about how bad a hurricane would be for people when it reached the land. Nowadays, satellites and radar towers collect this information and evaluating storms is much easier and safer. But some days I miss the thrill of being a storm chaser.

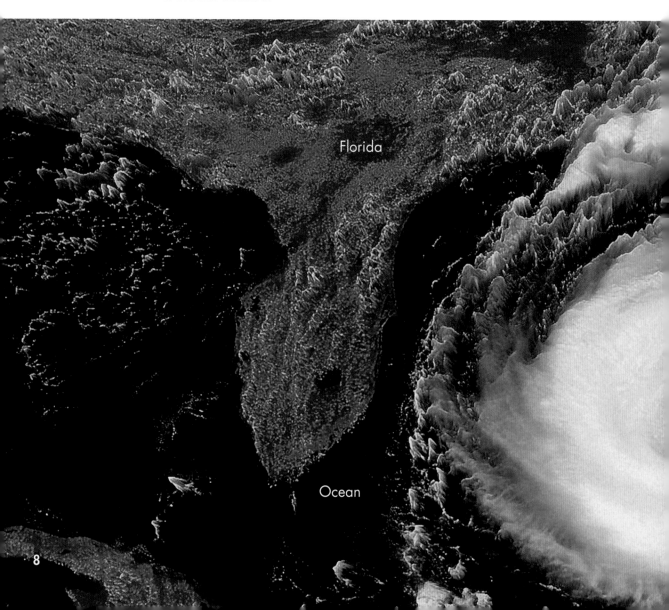

Florida

Ocean

Find out more

Find out about the Bureau of Meteorology. What does this organisation do? How is its storm data collected and analysed?

This is an aerial photograph of a hurricane approaching Florida.

Eye of hurricane

Find out how strong the wind is today

Wind can move silently, or it can roar. Make a wind chime so you can hear when the wind blows. Use your wind chime to remind you to observe the wind. Could you use it to predict a storm?

You will need:

- Ten small metal objects, such as bolts or screws
- Cotton or nylon thread of various lengths between 25 and 28 centimetres
- A pair of scissors
- A strong stick or twig about 30 centimetres long

1. Tie one end of a piece of thread to each object.
2. Tie the other end of each thread to the stick or twig so that the objects are hanging freely, approximately one centimetre apart from each other.
3. Tie two additional pieces of thread of the same length to each end of the stick or twig. Use these to hang your wind chime from a tree or other suitable place.

The wind pushes the objects and moves them. This makes them hit each other and shows that there is wind. When the objects hit each other, they make a sound. Listen and enjoy the music.

9

Find out more

What wild weather events have happened around the world lately? Describe the event and the damage caused.

Chapter 2

Extreme weather

Extreme weather conditions can have disastrous consequences. Power supplies can be cut off, roads may be blocked, and airports might need to be shut down. Sometimes many people have died as a result of severe weather. The places where some of the most devastating storms have occurred are marked on the map below. For more details, see pages 12 and 13.

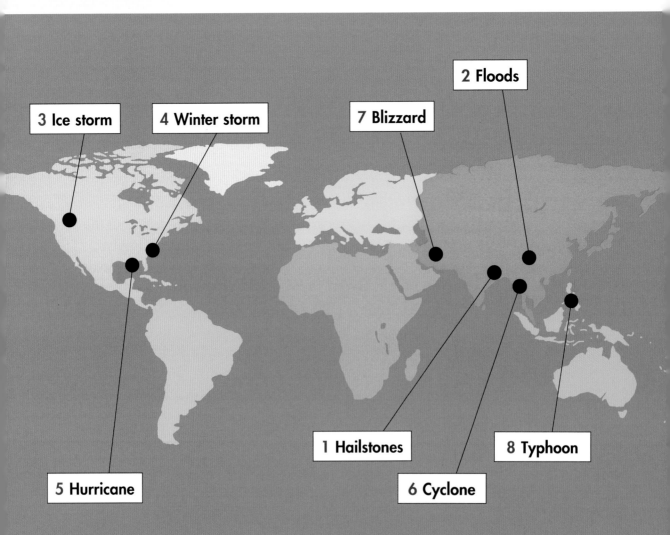

2 Floods

3 Ice storm

4 Winter storm

7 Blizzard

1 Hailstones

8 Typhoon

5 Hurricane

6 Cyclone

1 Hailstones

Place: Gopalganj, Bangladesh
Date: 14 April 1986
What happened? A storm produced 1 kilogram hailstones
Consequences: 92 people killed

2 Floods

Place: Southern China
Date: August 1931
What happened? Torrential rains caused the Yangtze River to flood
Consequences: 3.7 million people killed

3 Ice storm

Place: Canada and northern USA
Date: January 1998
What happened? Freezing rain fell for five days
Consequences: Airports, railways, roads closed; power cut off to more than three million people

4 Winter storm

Place: East coast, USA
Date: 12–13 March 1993
What happened? A storm swept across 26 states
Consequences: 500 people killed; about $1.2 billion in damage

5 Hurricane

Place: South coast, USA
Date: 25–29 August 2005
What happened? Hurricane Katrina struck
Consequences: 1,383 people killed; 1.5 million left homeless

6 Cyclone

Place: Irrawaddy River delta region, Myanmar
Date: 2–4 May 2008
What happened? Cyclone Nargis hit Myanmar
Consequences: 84,500 people killed; 37 townships devastated over two days

7 Blizzard

Place: Iran
Date: February 1972
What happened? A week-long blizzard ended a four-year drought
Consequences: 4,000 people killed

8 Typhoon

Place: Philippines
Date: November 1991
What happened? A typhoon caused flash flooding and landslides
Consequences: 6,000 people killed

Staying safe in extreme weather

Extreme weather can be frightening and dangerous. We need to be prepared for wild weather and to know what to do if we are caught in it. Families should prepare a plan so that everyone knows where to seek shelter and what to do when a storm is approaching, as well as what to do during and after a storm. Each type of storm requires different actions. To stay safe you will need to know what to do in each situation.

During and after a storm there may be no electricity, gas or water. Roads may be damaged and shops could be closed. This is why it is important to have an emergency kit. It will help you get through a storm and its aftermath.

After a storm, you may not know what damage has occurred, so listen to the radio or, if you can, watch TV to get news. You should only go outside with an adult, as it can be very dangerous – buildings may be unstable, power lines may be down and roads may have been washed away.

An emergency kit should contain:

- a first aid kit
- canned food and a manual can opener
- at least 15 litres of water per person
- protective clothing, bedding or sleeping bags
- battery-powered radio, torch and extra batteries
- any special items that your family may need, such as medicine, dust masks, baby food or food for your pets
- instructions on how to turn off electricity, gas and water if you need to do so.

Think about ...

What would you do to stay safe if wild weather happened where you live? How would you stay safe?

Did you know?

One of the most dangerous times is before a thunderstorm. Lightning can travel as far as 10 kilometres from a thundercloud, so lightning strikes can occur when the sky is still quite clear before a storm.

Chapter 3

Storms and survival

Thunderstorms

Thunderstorms occur all over the world at any time of the year. During these storms there is thunder and lightning. Lightning is **static electricity** that moves from cloud to cloud or from a cloud to the ground. Thunder is a loud, booming noise caused by the movement of lightning through the air. Lightning strikes can cause **bushfires** and hurt or kill living things, and can occur even before a storm hits. Thunderstorms can bring hail, heavy rain, flooding, strong winds and tornadoes.

SAFETY ADVICE

Remember the following things during a thunderstorm:

- If there are less than 30 seconds between seeing the lightning and hearing the thunder, there is a chance you could be struck by lightning. Seek shelter in a building.
- When indoors, stay away from large windows and metal doors, and do not use the telephone or take a bath or shower.
- If there are no buildings nearby, seek shelter in a car or truck (but not an open vehicle).
- If you are caught out in the open, avoid trees standing by themselves, hilltops and metal objects.
- Stay out of water and get off small boats.
- If your hair stands on end, your skin starts to tingle or you hear clicking sounds, lightning may be about to strike you. Get down on your hands and knees, and keep your head tucked in. Do not lie flat on the ground.

Tales of survival: Gina
Hit by lightning

Three years ago I was struck by lightning. I don't remember being hit. I woke up in the hospital with burns over a lot of my body. My eyes were burned, and my eyebrows and eyelashes were gone. Everything hurt.

I have kept the clothes I was wearing that day. My coat has a large black hole in the left shoulder. My pants and socks melted and look and feel like cardboard. My shoes blew up. I'm very lucky to be alive.

My heart stopped beating when I was hit, but there was a doctor nearby who was able to revive me.

Floods

Floods most often occur when a huge amount of rain falls in a short time. This can cause rivers to burst their banks and drainage systems to overflow. Flooding can also happen when tidal waves sweep across the land.

Floods can be very dangerous. As little as 15 centimetres of moving water is enough to wash a small car away. Water across a road can also hide washed-out footpaths. Floodwaters can also **inundate** buildings. Water seeping into the ground at the top of hills and cliffs can cause mudslides. Mudslides pick up rocks and trees and demolish houses and anything else in their way.

Flash floods

Flash floods can occur with little or no warning and reach full peak in only a few minutes. A flash flood can appear as a wave up to six metres high that moves as fast as an express train. It can tear trees from the ground and destroy buildings and bridges.

Think about ...
What would you do if floodwaters were rising around your house and a boat was coming to **evacuate** your house? What five items would you take with you? Why would you take these things?

Do the following when a flood is likely:

- Listen to a local radio station, watch the news on TV or check online for information and advice. If you are told to evacuate, you should do so as soon as possible.
- If flash flooding is likely, be ready to evacuate at a moment's notice.
- If a flash flood has already started, evacuate immediately.
- Move to higher ground away from rivers, streams and storm drains. Do not drive around barricades – they are there for your safety.
- Do not enter flood water.

Tales of survival: Hector
Rescue by boat

My family woke one morning to find that the river was flooded. Our house was surrounded by water. The water didn't come from the river itself but from the sewer, which had overflowed because of the flood. Throughout the day we watched as the brownish water crept over the kerb and moved slowly towards our house. By the time we went to bed, the water was lapping at the front steps. I was afraid to go to sleep. I thought that when I woke up, there would be water swirling across my bedroom floor. In the morning, the floodwater was still rising, so a man came in a boat and took us to the school hall. We stayed at the school for three days, until the flood went down. It took a long time to clean up the house and a lot of our things were ruined.

Hurricanes and cyclones

Hurricanes and cyclones are large, sometimes intensely violent tropical storms that build up over the ocean. When hurricanes and cyclones move over land, they bring winds of more than 120 kilometres per hour that can push over trees and send heavy objects flying through the air. They also bring torrential rain and huge waves that can cause flooding.

Storm surges

Hurricanes and cyclones can cause storm surges, where huge waves crash onto the shore and flood the land. A storm surge happens when high winds combine with low **air pressure** in the eye of a storm. The seawater is sucked up into a huge bulge, which the winds push towards the land. By the time the water has reached the coast, huge waves have formed. These break on the shore and either flood the land or wash the shore away. Storm surges are very dangerous because they happen with very little warning.

Did you know?

In Australia, a cyclone is a tropical storm that has winds of at least 63 kilometres per hour. In the United States, a hurricane is a tropical storm that has winds of at least 120 kilometres per hour. In Australia, this is called a severe tropical cyclone.

Find out more

Tropical storms, cyclones and hurricanes are given names to avoid confusion when more than one storm is happening at the same time. Find out about how the names for storms are chosen.

When a hurricane approaches:

- Listen to the radio and check for news on your phone and online. If you are told to evacuate, leave immediately and go to a safe place.

- If you are not advised to evacuate, stay indoors but away from windows.

- Watch for tornadoes, which can occur during or after a hurricane.

- Stay in the centre of the house, in a cupboard, or bathroom without windows.

- Stay away from floodwaters. If you are caught on a flooded road and the water is rising, get out of the car and climb to higher ground.

Tales of survival: the Spargo family
Hiding from a hurricane

Being in a hurricane is a frightening experience. One family huddled together in a small broom cupboard. When the storm had passed, they came out to find that most of their house and belongings had been blown away.

Mother: The worst part was being in the cupboard. It was small and we couldn't sit down because it was flooded.

Son: In the cupboard, we couldn't see what was happening. I got really scared when I heard the windows breaking.

Daughter: When I came out of the cupboard, I was very upset. The hurricane had completely wrecked our house.

Father: Our food blew away in the hurricane, too. We spent almost two days without anything to eat.

Find out more

Hurricanes and tornadoes are both wildly spinning winds. Find out what makes tornadoes and hurricanes different.

Tornadoes

Tornadoes are violently rotating columns of air that develop in thunderclouds and move down to the ground. They make so much noise that some people say they sound like 100 trains. Tornadoes have been known to have wind speeds of up to 500 kilometres per hour. They can toss cars through the air and rip up houses. Tornadoes are considered one of the most destructive forces on Earth. They usually accompany severe thunderstorms.

- The winds in tornadoes can gust at speeds of 500 kilometres per hour.
- Most tornadoes can be heard as a deafening roar from several kilometres away.
- Tornadoes are usually between 200 and 400 kilometres in diameter.
- The winds forming the funnel of a tornado generally move **anticlockwise** in the Northern Hemisphere and **clockwise** in the Southern Hemisphere.
- The air pressure at the centre of a tornado is much less than the air pressure outside it, which can cause buildings to explode.

Did you know?

Tornadoes are sometimes called twisters. They occur throughout the world, but are most intense and devastating in the United States. They most commonly occur in the afternoon or evening, after the heat of the day has produced the hot air necessary to cause a thunderstorm.

When a tornado is approaching, remember the following:

- If you are inside, go to a safe place to protect yourself from glass and other flying objects. You could go to your cellar or, if there is no cellar, a hallway in the middle of the house, or a bathroom or cupboard on the lowest floor. (This place should be kept uncluttered.)
- If you are outside, hurry to the cellar of a sturdy building nearby or lie flat in a ditch or low-lying area.
- If you are in a car or caravan, get out immediately and head for a safer place.

Tales of survival: Lucy
Terrifying tornado

The tornado came suddenly. There was dust everywhere and all kinds of objects were flying through the air. Dad told us to go down into the storm cellar right away. My little sister dropped everything and ran. My mother grabbed the cat and followed her. Dad and I were last down the stairs. Just as we closed the door behind us, we saw the corner of the house lift up. I could see light where the floor should have been. When we came out of the cellar, our house was gone – only the washing machine was left.

Sandstorms

Sandstorms occur mainly in the Middle East, North Africa, the United States, Australia and China. They usually form in deserts when strong winds pick up tonnes of sand and hurl it into the air. Sandstorms move very quickly and block out the light. They can reshape the land and bury buildings and cars. During sandstorms, the air is so full of sand that breathing is almost impossible.

Find out more

The simoom is a strong, dry wind full of sand that causes sandstorms in the Middle East and North Africa. The word *simoom* is Arabic. Find out what it means and why it is used to refer to this hot, dry wind.

The following advice will help keep you safe in a sandstorm or a dust storm.

- Seek shelter as soon as possible.
- Use a wet piece of cloth or a bandanna to cover your mouth and keep sand particles out of your lungs.
- Rub petroleum jelly along the inside of your nostrils to stop them from drying out.
- If you are outside with other people, make a human chain by linking elbows or holding hands to stay together.
- Move to higher ground (but not if the sandstorm is accompanied by a thunderstorm).
- If you are driving, pull off the road and onto the shoulder as far as possible. Turn off the car lights and set the emergency brakes.

Tales of survival: Andrés
Escape from a sandstorm

We had just finished setting up camp when I spotted a large, dark cloud across the sand dunes. It was heading straight towards us and was moving very quickly. Everything above and below it was black, as if someone had turned off the lights behind it. "Sandstorm," I yelled. We ran to the Jeep with the raging wall of sand bearing down on us. We just had time to slam the doors shut before it overwhelmed us. Outside, it was very dark. The Jeep was pelted with sand and small rocks. We had to sit and wait until the storm passed. Hours later, when it was safe to get out of the Jeep, we found that one side of it was almost buried in sand. All our camping gear was gone.

Chapter 4

Extreme heat and freezing cold

Heat wave continues

13 January 2016

Record high temperatures are predicted today as the heat wave enters its fifth day, once again bringing blistering heat to our city.

The Weather Bureau has forecast a top temperature of 45° Celsius, with an overnight low of 30° Celsius, and emergency services are on alert.

Emergency departments around the city report that hundreds of patients are arriving with heat-related illnesses. Six deaths have been caused by the hot weather.

Dr Susan Melling, an emergency medicine specialist, warned that very hot weather was extremely dangerous.

"It can lead to **dehydration** and **heat stroke** and is sometimes fatal," Dr Melling said. "Old people and babies are more likely to suffer from the heat."

Dr Melling said people should stay indoors as much as possible, avoid too much exercise and drink two or more glasses of water every hour.

She also recommended the following precautions:

- Stay in air-conditioned buildings whenever possible.
- If you have to be outside, stay in the shade and wear protective clothing and sunscreen.
- If you have to work outside, use a buddy system and check on each other every hour or so. If your buddy becomes confused or loses consciousness, seek medical help straight away as they may be suffering from heat stroke.

The Weather Bureau predicts that the hot weather will continue for at least three more days.

Staying safe in the heat

What should people do to stay safe in extremely hot weather?

The biggest danger in hot weather is the loss of body fluids. When a person's body becomes too hot, he or she can become dehydrated. Dehydration means that the body is losing fluid faster than it is being replaced by drinking.

If a person loses too much fluid, his or her temperature may start to rise quickly, as the body cannot cool itself. This is called heat stroke, and it can cause damage to your brain or other vital organs, and even be fatal.

What safety steps should people follow during hot weather?

You should:

- drink plenty of water
- avoid sugary or alcoholic drinks, because these actually cause your body to lose more fluid
- stay indoors if possible
- wear a broad-brimmed hat and sunscreen, and stay out of the sun if you are outside
- wear light-coloured, lightweight, loose clothing
- avoid too much activity
- never leave anyone, especially a young child, in a parked car.

Caught in a blizzard

14 January 2016

The past 24 hours have brought freezing rain, blizzards and severe snowstorms to the whole city and surrounding countryside. Thirty-two people needed emergency assistance when they became trapped in their cars on the freeway.

Early this morning it was discovered that a school bus had run off Lake Road and become stuck in a snowdrift. It had been there for 26 hours. Sali Ibrahim was one of the children on the bus. He told his story to the *Morning Star.*

"We were still quite a long way from school when the bus slid on some ice and ended up in a ditch. Everyone was screaming and crying. After a while, we realised that we were stranded. The engine wouldn't start and it was soon freezing cold. We jumped around to try and keep warm, but got really tired. It got so cold that our lunches froze, so we had nothing to eat or drink. After a few hours, the bus driver went for help. He hadn't returned by the time it was dark. Then it got even colder. We huddled together to try and keep warm. When morning came and we heard the rescuers digging the bus out, we all cheered and cried."

All the children survived, but seven had frostbitten toes and several received minor cuts and scratches in the crash. The bus driver was found frozen to death about a kilometre from the bus. His name has not yet been released.

Staying safe in the cold

What should people do to stay safe in extremely cold weather?

The biggest danger in cold weather is loss of body heat. When a person loses too much body heat, he or she can become hypothermic. People with **hypothermia** can become very **disoriented** and so can easily get lost. It is important to wear warm clothing and stay out of the wind. Lots of thin layers of clothes are warmer than one or two thicker items. People should also wear mittens and a hat and scarf. The top layer of clothing should be waterproof.

What safety steps should people follow during an ice storm, snowstorm or blizzard?

You should:

- stay indoors and keep warm
- wear suitable clothing
- have plenty of warm blankets on hand in case heating is not available
- if forced to go outside, walk carefully on snowy, icy footpaths
- listen to the radio, watch TV or check online for up-to-date weather information.

Find out more

An ice storm is a storm that produces more than six centimetres of ice during freezing rains. Ice storms are one of the most dangerous forms of weather. Find out more about ice storms. How much freezing rain is needed to produce enough ice for an ice storm? How can ice storms have an impact on people?

Sometimes a blizzard will strike without much warning. What should people do if they are caught in their car during a blizzard?

If you get caught in your car, you should:

- Stay with your car. Do not try to walk to safety. Keep an emergency kit in your car that includes blankets, a torch, a battery-operated radio, some water and some chocolate.
- Tie a brightly coloured cloth (preferably red) to the car's exterior for rescuers to see.
- Start the car and use the heater for about 10 minutes every hour. Keep the exhaust pipe clear so fumes don't back up in the car.
- Leave the overhead light on when the engine is running so that the car can be seen.
- As you sit, move your arms and legs to keep blood circulating and to stay warm.
- Keep a window away from the wind slightly open to let in air.

Did you know?

Frostbite occurs when the skin and sometimes the tissue under the skin freeze in very cold weather. Frostbite most commonly affects the hands, feet, ears, nose and face. Very serious cases of frostbite can result in amputation.

Glossary

air pressure when air pushes on the surfaces it touches, or the force exerted on you by the weight of air

anticlockwise moving in the opposite direction as the hands of a clock

bushfires raging fires that spread very quickly

clockwise moving in the same direction as the hands of a clock

dehydration when fluid is being lost from the body faster than it is being replaced by drinking

disoriented confused about where you are; lost

evacuate remove people from a dangerous place

heat stroke when the body's temperature rises due to dehydration

hypothermia when body temperature drops to a dangerously low level

inundate to cover with a flood

meteorologist a scientist who studies weather and makes weather predictions

static electricity an electrical charge that builds up on a surface and is released into the air

Index